WHAT DO THEY DO?

PRINCIPALS

BY GAETANO CAPICI

CHERRY LAKE Publishing

Published in the United States of America by Cherry Lake Publishing
Ann Arbor, Michigan
www.cherrylakepublishing.com

Content Adviser: W. Diane Cargile, Ed.D., President, National Association of Elementary School Principals
Reading Adviser: Cecilia Minden-Cupp, PhD, Literacy Consultant

Photo Credits: Cover and page 1, ©iStockphoto.com/Willie B. Thomas; page 5, ©ACE STOCK LIMITED/Alamy; page 7, ©Jeff Greenberg/Alamy; page 9, ©Pixart/Dreamstime.com; page 11, ©kristian sekulic, used under license from Shutterstock, Inc.; page 13, ©iStockphoto.com/nano; page 15, ©Marmaduke St. John/Alamy; page 17, ©iStockphoto.com/sjlocke; page 19, ©Feverpitch, used under license from Shutterstock, Inc.; page 21, ©iStockphoto.com/wbritten

LIBRARY OF CONGRESS CATALOGING-IN-PUBLICATION DATA
Capici, Gaetano, 1985–
What do they do? Principals / by Gaetano Capici.
p. cm.—(Community connections)
Includes bibliographical references and index.
ISBN-13: 978-1-60279-809-0 (lib. bdg.)
ISBN-10: 1-60279-809-5 (lib. bdg.)
1. School principals—Professional relationships. 2. Educational leadership. 3. School personnel management. I. Title.
LB2831.9.C36 2011
371.2'012—dc22 2009042805

Cherry Lake Publishing would like to acknowledge the work of The Partnership for 21st Century Skills. Please visit *www.21stcenturyskills.org* for more information.

Printed in the United States of America
Corporate Graphics Inc.
August 2011
CLFA07

PRINCIPALS

CONTENTS

SCHOOL LEADERS

The crowd claps. You and your classmates take a bow. The school play was a big hit. You spot your family and teachers. There is also another person cheering everyone on. It is the principal!

Principals are school leaders. They have very important jobs.

Have you been in a school play? School principals encourage everyone to take part.

Principals make sure that every school day goes well. They help set up rules. These rules keep students safe.

Sometimes people break the rules. The principal explains to them why rules are important. She may also speak with classmates who don't get along. Principals try to meet the needs of all students.

Principals help students understand the importance of rules.

Principals also do fun things with students. They cheer on sports teams. They greet students at the start of each day. They sometimes read to students. Principals want everyone to feel safe and happy at school.

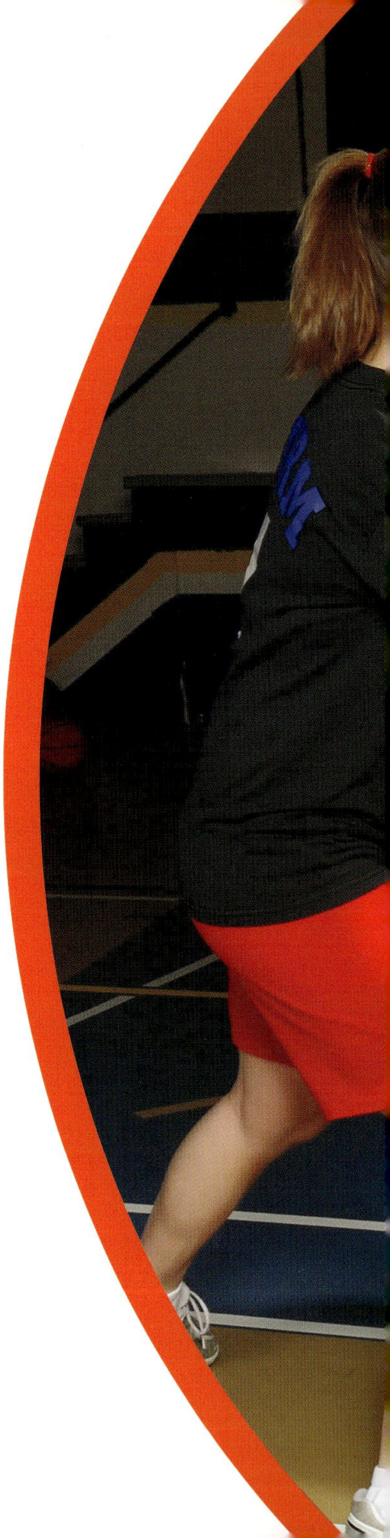

Principals cheer at basketball games!

LOOK!

Principals enjoy spending time with students. Be on the lookout for your school principal. How many times can you spot her in one week? Where do you see her? Is she in the hallway or at recess? Did you look in the lunchroom?

PART OF A TEAM

Principals want the best workers at their schools. They hire great teachers. They hire people who keep the school clean. They hire cooks for the lunchroom. They also hire people who work in the office.

Principals try to hire the best teachers.

THINK!

Did you know that many principals started out as teachers? Think about it. How might teaching help someone become a good principal? Hint: Do teachers spend a lot of time with students? Do they need to be good leaders?

Principals often visit classrooms. They **observe** teachers. Principals give teachers tips on how to **improve**.

Principals and teachers work as a team. They work together to plan **lessons**.

Principals also look at test scores. They find ways to help students do better.

Principals offer advice to students.

A principal spends a lot of time in classrooms and hallways. He also meets with parents. He answers e-mails.

Principals find the best ways to use the school's **budget**. They decide what supplies are needed. They also find ways to raise more money.

Principals might spend time with students during lunch.

Principals have some important helpers. Some people help in the school office. They answer phones. They keep track of the day's activities.

Assistant principals also help. They may plan programs for the school. Principals must work well with everyone.

Assistant principals plan programs at school.

COMMUNITY LEADERS

Principals also speak with people in the **community**. They work with businesses. These businesses help the school.

Principals may show a new family around the school. They will talk to the family and make them feel welcome.

New families are welcomed by principals and teachers.

CREATE!

Pretend you are a news reporter. Your job is to write about principals. Discover five things that they do on the job. Try asking your principal for more facts about his work. Now share your writing with a friend. What did your friend think of your ideas?

Running a school is not easy. Principals work long hours. They often work on weekends. Sometimes they must deal with unhappy parents or teachers.

Remember that all principals were students at one time. They care about everyone at school. They want you to learn and be safe!

Principals work hard to make their schools the best they can be.

GLOSSARY

assistant (uh-SISS-tuhnt) acting as a helper or having to do with helping another person

budget (BUHJ-it) a plan of how money will be earned and the ways it will be spent

community (kuh-MYOO-nuh-tee) a group of people who live in the same area; also, the area itself

improve (im-PROOV) to get better or make something better

lessons (LESS-uhnz) sets of information that are learned, studied, or taught

observe (uhb-ZURV) to watch closely and carefully

FIND OUT MORE

BOOKS

Marsico, Katie. *Working at a School.* Ann Arbor, MI: Cherry Lake Publishing, 2009.

Mitchell, Melanie. *Principals.* Minneapolis: Lerner Publications Company, 2005.

WEB SITES

National Association of Elementary School Principals
www.naesp.org/
Learn more about principals and their responsibilities.

PBS Kids—Middle School: A Principal's Advice
pbskids.org/itsmylife/school/middleschool/article5.html
Middle school is only a few years away. Find tips from an elementary school principal about making the switch.

INDEX

ABOUT THE AUTHOR

Gaetano Capici graduated from DePaul University with bachelor's degrees in English and Spanish. He lives near Chicago, Illinois. He would like to thank all principals for their countless hours of hard work and dedication.